U.S. Fish & Wildlife Service

Rising to the Urgent Challenge

Strategic Plan for Responding to Accelerating Climate Change

U.S. Fish & Wildlife Service

*We must act now,
as if the future
of fish and wildlife
and people
hangs in the balance —
for indeed,
all indications are
that it does.*

On the cover: *Polar bears.
Courtesy of National Geographic
Society.*

Table of Contents

Executive Overview

THE U.S. FISH AND WILDLIFE SERVICE (SERVICE) IS AN AGENCY BORN OF ECOLOGICAL CRISIS and raised on the nation's will to respond. The Service's genesis was the Federal response in 1871 to the collapse in the nation's food fishes from overharvesting, and its mandate was to find ways to reverse that decline. By the early 1900s, a crisis over the decimation of migratory birds for their plumes prompted the development of a national system of lands and waters set aside as refuges for wildlife and the passage of the first Federal wildlife laws. By the mid-1960s, the loss and threat of loss of species of fish and wildlife[a] from human-induced pressures grew the Service's mission to also include the conservation and recovery of threatened and endangered species.

Over its 139-year history, the Service has faced every challenge to the future of the nation's fish and wildlife heritage head-on. As an agency within the Department of the Interior (Department), we have attracted to our ranks those individuals whose personal commitment to conserving, protecting, and enhancing America's fish and wildlife resources is matched by their professional resolve to do whatever it takes to accomplish that mission. The passion and creativity that drove Spencer Baird, Paul Kroegel, Guy Bradley, J.N. "Ding" Darling, Rachel Carson and countless others who have stood in the breach for wildlife lives on in the hearts and minds of today's Fish and Wildlife Service employees.

At the dawn of the 21st century, we find our commitment and resolve and our passion and creativity being called upon once again as we face what portends to be the greatest challenge to fish and wildlife conservation in the history of the Service: The Earth's climate is changing at an accelerating rate that has the potential to cause abrupt changes in ecosystems and increase the risk of species extinctions. In turn, these changes will adversely affect local, State, Tribal, regional, national and international economies and cultures; and will diminish the goods, services, and social benefits that we Americans are accustomed to receiving, at little cost to ourselves, from ecosystems across our nation.

Given the disruption that a changing climate implies for our mission, our nation, and our world, we in the Service and the Department cannot afford to simply give lip service to this crisis and go on about business as usual. We are at a crossroads in our nation's conservation history. We must rise up and respond to a 21st century conservation challenge with 21st century organizational, managerial, and scientific tools and approaches. To address and combat climate change and its impacts, we must position the Service more strategically for this battle. We must build shared scientific and technical capabilities with others and work more collaboratively than ever before with the conservation community[b], in particular, our State and Tribal partners, who share direct responsibility for managing our nation's wildlife resources.

A diver monitors coral reef health at the FWS-managed Palmyra Atoll National Wildlife Refuge. Photo: J. Maragos / USFWS

---

a Our use of the term **fish and wildlife** throughout this plan includes fish, wildlife, and plants, and the habitats upon which all three depend.

b The **conservation community** includes governments, business and industry, non-governmental organizations, academia, private landowners, and citizens who are interested and active in conservation efforts.

As a Service and Department we must act decisively, recognizing that climate change threatens to exacerbate other existing pressures on the sustainability of our fish and wildlife resources. We must act boldly, without having all the answers, confident that we will learn and adapt as we go. And most importantly, we must act now, as if the future of fish and wildlife and people hangs in the balance—for indeed, all indications are that it does.

As a Service, we are committed to examining everything we do, every decision we make, and every dollar we spend through the lens of climate change, fully confident in our workforce to rise to this challenge and to lead from in front and from behind. We recognize their efforts that are already underway, and we look to our employees for their on-the-ground knowledge and expertise in focusing our energies and recalibrating our activities.

Our Strategic Plan acknowledges that no single organization or agency can address an environmental challenge of such global proportions without allying itself with others in partnerships across the nation and around the world. This document commits us to a philosophy of interdependent, collaborative conservation, rooted in our **Climate Change Principles** (see sidebar, page 2).

Individual commitment to a group effort — that is what makes a team work, a company work, a society work, a civilization work.

VINCE LOMBARDI, 1913–1970, American football coach and national symbol of single-minded determination to win

Our Strategic Plan's primary purposes are to (1) lay out our vision for accomplishing our mission to "work with others to conserve, protect, and enhance fish, wildlife, and plants and their habitats for the continuing benefit of the American people" in the face of accelerating climate change; and (2) provide direction for our own organization and its employees, defining our role within the context of the Department of the Interior and the larger conservation community. In this plan, we express our commitment to our vision through strategic goals and objectives that we believe must be accomplished to sustain fish and wildlife nationally and internationally. In an appended **5-Year Action Plan for Implementing the Climate Change Strategic Plan**, we identify specific actions that will lead to the accomplishment of our goals and objectives.

Tide Returns to Nisqually Estuary

River delta restoration projects are considered crucial to provide increased resiliency to large estuary systems and illustrate a tool for adaptation in the face of climate change and related impacts of sea level rise. After a century of diking off tidal flow, the Brown Farm Dike was removed to inundate 762 acres of Nisqually (WA) National Wildlife Refuge in October 2009. Along with 140 acres of tidal wetlands restored by the Nisqually Indian Tribe, the Nisqually Delta represents the largest tidal marsh restoration project in the Pacific Northwest to assist in recovery of Puget Sound salmon and wildlife populations. During the past decade, the refuge and close partners, including the Tribe and Ducks Unlimited, have restored more than 22 miles of the historic tidal slough systems and re-connected historic floodplains to the Puget Sound in Washington, increasing potential salt marsh habitat in the southern reach of Puget Sound by 50 percent. The project also restored 25 acres of riparian surge plain forest, an extremely depleted type of tidal forest important for juvenile salmon and songbirds.

Restoration of the Nisqually estuary is an adaptation approach that helps promote system resiliency to climate change effects such as:

- Increased winter storms, rainfall, and flooding
- Loss of forest cover due to increases in insect infestations and fire
- Rise in sea level resulting in loss of shoreline areas
- Loss of habitats and biodiversity

(Above) Nisqually estuary. Photo: USFWS

The goals and objectives of our Strategic Plan are nested
under three major strategies:

Adaptation: Minimizing the impact of climate change on fish and wildlife through the application of cutting-edge science in managing species and habitats.

Mitigation: Reducing levels of greenhouse gases in the Earth's atmosphere.

Engagement: Joining forces with others to seek solutions to the challenges and threats to fish and wildlife conservation posed by climate change.

Federal and State biologists survey aquatic resources to document the effects of changing temperatures and water quality.

We recognize that as an organization, the Service has been entrusted by the American people with legal authorities for fish and wildlife conservation that are national and international in scope and that put us in a position of unique responsibility within the conservation community. These authorities and responsibilities include working across jurisdictional boundaries in shared responsibility with all 50 States to manage fish and wildlife populations; conserving endangered and threatened species, inter-jurisdictional fish, and migratory birds; managing an unequaled conservation land base, the 150-million-acre National Wildlife Refuge System; and collaborating in carrying out conservation activities internationally through conventions, treaties, and agreements with foreign nations.

By virtue of this public trust, the Service accepts its obligation to take leadership in helping to catalyze the conservation community's collective response to climate change. We will bring the community together to engage in dialogue; identify common interests and goals; and define innovative, collaborative, and effective strategies for addressing this shared crisis. We recognize that our own future success in conserving fish and wildlife will depend on how well we integrate our efforts with those of our partners, how quickly we can build needed technical and technological capacities and capabilities, and how strategic we are with our limited resources in addressing climate-induced changes.

Our Strategic Plan acknowledges the climate crisis as one of enormous consequence and challenge for fish and wildlife conservation. We put this plan forward as a manifestation of our resolve, as individuals and as an organization, to face this challenge with a sense of duty and integrity, and a spirit of public service and optimism.

Our Vision

OVER THE 21st CENTURY, THE U.S. FISH AND WILDLIFE SERVICE AND THE DEPARTMENT OF THE INTERIOR ENVISION a North American continent continuing to be altered by accelerating climate change, but managed to sustain diverse, distributed, and abundant populations of fish and wildlife through conservation of healthy habitats in a network of interconnected, ecologically functioning[c] landscapes.

While many species will continue to thrive, we also envision that some populations and species may decline or be lost, and some will only survive in the wild through our direct and continuous intervention. We will be especially challenged to conserve species and habitats that are particularly vulnerable[d] to climate-driven changes, but we will dedicate our absolute best efforts and expertise to the task, understanding fully that we must continue to meet our obligations for conserving trust species. We will need to make choices and set priorities and, working with our partners, apply ourselves where we can make the greatest difference.

We see climate change as an issue that will unite the conservation community like no other issue has since the early 1960s, when Rachel Carson sounded an alarm about pesticides. We envision a new era of collaborative conservation in which members of the conservation community work interdependently, building knowledge, sharing expertise, and pooling resources as we craft explicit landscape-scale goals and pursue these goals together. We foresee unparalleled opportunities to engage with, and enlist the involvement of, private citizens, businesses and industry, non-governmental organizations, and national and international governments at all levels to conserve fish and wildlife in the face of climate change.

Rising Sea Levels on North Carolina Coast

North Carolina's east coast is identified as particularly vulnerable to climate change because it is so long, low and flat. As rising sea levels have pushed saltwater into the area, peat soils are degrading and plants and trees have died. Researchers estimate that 1 million acres along the coast could be lost within 100 years.

We know that the estuarine waters surrounding Alligator River National Wildlife Refuge are getting saltier. We've seen with our own eyes shoreline losses and plant community changes on thousands of acres of this 153,000-acre Refuge. Modeling data suggests that if nothing is done, we'll lose up to 67 percent of swamp land and 90 of dry land by 2100 — that's most of the Refuge.

We're finding opportunities in the crisis. We're working with The Nature Conservancy, Duke Energy, and other partners to create a management response that includes building resilience into the land and connecting Refuge lands to other lands. Duke Energy donated $1 million that will fund climate change research and activities to help wildlife adapt to the effects of rising sea levels on the Refuge.

MIKE BRYANT, *Project Leader, North Carolina Coastal Plain Refuges Complex, Manteo, NC*

(Above) Saltwater intrusion is affecting plant life at Alligator River NWR. Photo: Debbie Crane / The Nature Conservancy

---

c **Ecologically-functioning** landscapes are those in which key ecological processes (such as disturbance regimes) are maintained or restored to promote resilience to climate change.

d According to the IPCC, **vulnerability** is the degree to which a system is susceptible to, or unable to cope with, adverse effects of climate change, including climate variability and extremes. It is a function of the sensitivity of a particular system to climate changes, its exposure to those changes, and its capacity to adapt to those changes.

Introduction

CLIMATE CHANGE IS AN IMMENSE, SERIOUS, AND SOBERING CHALLENGE — one that will affect fish and wildlife profoundly. At the same time, climate change is galvanizing the conservation community in ways we have not seen since a half-century ago, when *Silent Spring* alerted the world to the hazards of overuse of pesticides and launched a worldwide environmental movement.

As concern for climate change and its impacts grows, so do the opportunities for the Service and members of the conservation community to pool our talents, imagination, creativity, and spirit of public service to reduce and manage those impacts in ways that sustain fish and wildlife. Working interdependently and collaboratively, the Service will mount a bold response to climate change, on the ground, where our actions have the most impact; and in other settings where policies, priorities, and budgets are shaped and tough choices and decisions are made.

Across the Service, our employees have initiated action to address climate change. Some employees are monitoring sea level rise and exploring ways of safeguarding our coastal National Wildlife Refuges and the trust resources they support. Others are working tirelessly with water managers to ensure fish and wildlife resources are considered meaningfully in water allocation decisions, particularly in the Southwest, where climate change is likely to exacerbate drought. Some are busy calculating the Service's carbon footprint[e] and devising innovative ways to help the Service become carbon neutral[f]. Still other employees are reaching out to our workforce and our external partners to help them better understand the direction and magnitude of climate change and its effects on fish and wildlife.

It remains for the Service to do two things: First, we must focus the talents, creativity and energy of our employees on a common set of strategies, goals, objectives and actions for addressing climate change impacts. Second, we must provide employees with additional support in terms of knowledge, technology, and resources to enable them to realize their full potential in conserving fish and wildlife in the face of climate change.

This Strategic Plan establishes a basic framework within which the U.S. Fish and Wildlife Service will work as part of a broader, Department-wide strategy[g] and with the larger conservation community (especially States and Tribes as entities with formal wildlife management responsibilities) to help ensure the sustainability of fish and wildlife in light of accelerating climate change. The plan looks broadly at how climate change is affecting these resources; what our role will be as a key member of the conservation community with national responsibilities for fish and wildlife conservation; and what we will contribute to the international community and its campaign to ensure the future of fish and wildlife globally.

This plan is a starting point for action and discussion. It was drafted by a team of Service employees representing all regions and programs, and has been revised to reflect the thousands of comments from Service employees and members of the public. We look forward to updating it further as we work with and learn from others, as our experiences and knowledge grow, and as the conservation community unites more closely in a new era of collaborative conservation.

Did You Know...

■ In the Arctic, record losses of sea ice over the past decade are affecting the distribution, behavior, and abundance of polar bears, animals that are almost completely dependent upon sea ice for survival.

■ In the Southeast, rising sea levels are expected to flood as much as 30 percent of the habitat on the Service's coastal Refuges.

■ In the Southwest, climate change is already exacerbating deep droughts, increasing pressure on water uses at the Service's National Fish Hatcheries and National Wildlife Refuges.

■ In the Northwest, climate change is warming the landscape and enabling insect pests to expand their ranges and destroy ecologically and commercially valuable forests.

---

e A **carbon footprint** is typically defined as "the total set of GHG (greenhouse gas) emissions caused directly and indirectly by an individual, organization, event or product" (UK Carbon Trust 2008).

f Being **carbon neutral** is typically defined as having a net zero carbon footprint, i.e., achieving net zero carbon emissions by balancing a measured amount of carbon released with an equivalent amount that is sequestered or offset.

g The **Department's climate change strategy** is described in Secretarial Order 3289 <elips.doi.gov/app_so/act_getfiles.cfm?order_number=3289A1>.

The Crisis

"**WARMING OF THE CLIMATE SYSTEM IS UNEQUIVOCAL,** as is now evident from observations of increases in global average air and ocean temperatures, widespread melting of snow and ice, and rising global average sea level. ... Most of the observed increase in global average temperatures since the mid-20th century is very likely due to the observed increase in anthropogenic greenhouse gas concentrations." So concludes the Intergovernmental Panel on Climate Change (IPCC) in its *Fourth Assessment Report* published in 2007[1]. There is no longer any doubt that the Earth's climate is changing at an accelerating rate and that the changes are largely the result of human-generated greenhouse gas concentrations in the atmosphere caused by increasing human development and population growth. Climate change has manifested itself in rising sea levels, melting sea ice and glaciers, changing precipitation patterns, growing frequency and severity of storms, and increasing ocean acidification.

A growing body of evidence has linked accelerating climate change[h] with observed changes in fish and wildlife, their populations, and their habitats in the United States[2]. Polar bear population declines have already been noted in Canada[3], and extirpations of Bay checkerspot butterfly populations in the San Francisco Bay[4] area are also documented. Across the continental United States, climate change is affecting the migration cycles and body condition of migratory songbirds, causing decoupling of the arrival dates of birds on their breeding grounds and the availability of the food they need for successful reproduction[5].

Climate change has very likely increased the size and number of wildfires, insect outbreaks, pathogens, disease outbreaks, and tree mortality in the interior West, the Southwest, and Alaska and will continue to do so.[2] In the aquatic environment, evidence is growing that higher water temperatures resulting from climate change are negatively impacting cold- and cool-water fish populations across the country[6]. Along our coasts, rising sea levels have begun to affect fish and wildlife habitats, including those used by shorebirds and sea turtles that nest on our coastal National Wildlife Refuges[7]. In the oceans, subtropical and tropical corals in shallow waters have already suffered major bleaching events driven by increases in sea surface temperatures.[2]

The immensity and urgency of the climate change challenge are indeed sobering. The IPCC's *Fourth Assessment Report*[1] estimates that approximately 20–30 percent of the world's plant and animal species assessed as of 2006 are likely to be at increasingly high risk of extinction as global mean temperatures exceed a warming of 2–3°C above preindustrial levels. Global average temperature increases of 0.74°C are already documented, and temperature increases in some areas are projected to exceed 3.0°C over the next decade. The IPCC further concludes that substantial changes in structure and functioning of terrestrial ecosystems are very likely to occur with a global warming of more than 2–3°C above pre-industrial levels. These changes will have predominantly negative consequences for biodiversity and ecosystem goods and services (e.g., water and food).

The IPCC also reports that the resilience of many ecosystems around the world is likely to be exceeded this century by an unprecedented combination of climate change; disturbances associated with climate change, such as flooding, drought, wildfire, and insects; and other global change-drivers, including land-use changes, pollution, habitat fragmentation, urbanization, and growing human populations and economies. These projected changes have enormous implications for management of fish and wildlife and their habitats around the world.

Climate change has the potential to cause abrupt ecosystem changes and increased species extinctions. These changes will reduce the ability of natural systems to provide many societal goods and services—including the availability of clean water, our planet's lifeblood—which in turn will impact local, regional, and national economies and cultures. Clearly, we cannot delay in addressing climate change effects on fish and wildlife. They demand urgent attention and aggressive action.

---

h Hereafter, when we refer to **climate change**, we mean accelerating climate change. While climate change has occurred throughout the history of our planet, current changes are occurring at a greatly accelerated rate, largely as a result of human activities.

The Challenge

MISSION SUCCESS IN FISH AND WILDLIFE CONSERVATION OVER THE COMING DECADES WILL REQUIRE UNPRECEDENTED COOPERATION and partnership among governments, private sector and non-government organizations, and individual citizens. Consequently, the greatest challenge we and other members of the conservation community face is the need to form new and interdependent relationships, sharing integrated capacities, building on common strengths, identifying and addressing weaknesses, and focusing our responses on shared goals and objectives. For the Service, this is especially true of our relationships with State fish and wildlife agencies, which have management authority on much of our nation's lands and waters; and with Tribal fish and wildlife management authorities.

Effect of Warmer Winters On Spring Snowpack and Summer Stream-flows

In the Klamath Basin of southern Oregon, spring snowpack represents a reservoir of water that will sustain stream-flows throughout the summer. In recent years, warmer winters have resulted in more precipitation falling as rain instead of snow, reducing the spring snowpack. Rivers in the upper Basin have shown rather large declines in stream inflows in recent decades. This includes inflows to Upper Klamath Lake that provide water for irrigation, National Wildlife Refuges, sucker habitat, and downstream river-flows for salmon.

This trend means that in the Klamath Basin, as elsewhere, we can no longer assume that the future will look like the past. As warming trends continue, there will be less water available to meet competing demands. Like many water issues in the West, resolution of water issues in the Klamath Basin will require landscape-scale solutions and the active involvement and cooperation of all stakeholders.

TIM MAYER, *Water Resources Branch Hydrologist, Engineering Division, Portland, OR*

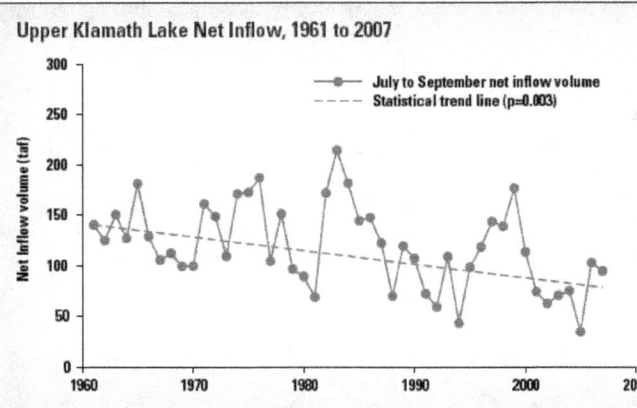

Upper Klamath Lake Net Inflow, 1961 to 2007

This graph shows the actual measurements of net inflows. The dashed statistical-trend line indicates that despite some variability from year to year, there has been a downward trend from July–Sept. since 1961.

To succeed in sustaining fish and wildlife, our plans and actions must recognize all management roles and authorities and realistically reflect the limitations and uncertainties in our understanding of climate change. They must target stewardship activities at all geographic scales, beginning with the design of conservation strategies at landscape scales. Our plans and actions must also encourage collaborative approaches that give common purpose to our employees and our conservation activities at local, State, regional, national, continental, international, and global levels.

Our experiences with climate change, such as the effect of sea ice changes on polar bears, have taught us that we will be increasingly challenged to recalibrate our conservation goals by integrating climate change. We need to plan for conservation on landscape scales and be prepared to act quickly, sometimes without the scientific certainty we would prefer.

Climate change is the transformational conservation challenge of our time, not only because of its direct effects, but also because of its influence on the other stressors that have been and will continue to be major conservation priorities.

Many other issues, such as the spread and control of invasive species; the mounting pressures on limited water supplies; the need for robust fire management to help conserve natural systems; the harm to species from exposure to environmental contaminants; continued changes in land use, specifically habitat loss; and the impacts of all of these factors on biodiversity, have been and will continue to pose tremendous challenges to sustaining healthy, vibrant ecosystems.

*Climate change is the transformational
conservation challenge of our time*

Climate change does not replace these other threats or render them less important; they must remain priorities in the years ahead. It is, however, essential that we understand how climate change will exacerbate these threats and pose new ones. For example, climate change will allow the range of some invasive species to expand, perhaps markedly. Climate change will also make some regions drier, further complicating what are already very challenging efforts to capture water and deliver it to natural systems. These changes in precipitation patterns will also affect fire regimes. Our employees and partners will need to take this into account in their management activities so as to protect both the natural world and the places where people live.

In addition, climate change will have many unforeseen impacts on land use and development. For example, rising seas will result in immense pressure to build sea walls and other structures to protect coastal development. These actions will impact the fish and wildlife that rely upon nearby beaches, salt marshes and other natural habitats. Furthermore, climate change may divert development pressure from coastal areas to relatively higher ground as people seek to escape places threatened by rising seas. Together, all of these stressors will have impacts on species that are imperiled today, and they could cause others to become imperiled for the first time.

Future Impacts Are Uncertain

One of the major challenges of addressing climate change effects on fish and wildlife is identifying and addressing uncertainty[i] in our understanding of future climate change and how that change will affect ecological systems. Our understanding of future climate change is based largely on projections from global climate models (also known as General Circulation Models) that are run using different greenhouse gas emissions scenarios developed by the IPCC. These projections contain a degree of uncertainty resulting from the inability of climate models to perfectly simulate the climate system, particularly at regional geographic scales and less than decadal time intervals; and uncertainty over which greenhouse gas emissions scenario will be realized in the future. As the IPCC has stated, the emissions scenarios are "based on assumptions concerning... future socio-economic and technological developments that may or may not be realized, and are therefore subject to substantial uncertainty." There also remains much uncertainty over how climate change will affect ecological systems at different scales, especially in its interactions with such non-climate stressors as land-use changes.

Finally, unanticipated impacts of climate change have already occurred and are likely to occur in the future. These impacts are difficult to predict based on our current understanding of climate and ecological systems, adding further uncertainty to our ability to predict the future. We must account for this uncertainty as we design, implement and evaluate our plans in response to climate change and as we carry out our management, regulatory and monitoring programs. We must learn as we go, using new knowledge and results of focused research to reduce uncertainty. As we learn more about climate change, we will be better able to refine our planning, decisions, and management actions to reflect that greater understanding.

The Challenge of Thinking Differently about Partnerships

In the Southeast, we have built new relationships with traditional and non-traditional partners—The Conservation Fund, American Electric Power Company, and Entergy Inc.—to help achieve their objectives and ours. Nine years ago, we launched an innovative program in the Lower Mississippi Valley aimed at restoring native habitats to bolster populations of wildlife and migratory birds through a carbon sequestration initiative. Together we have added more than 40,000 acres of habitat to the National Wildlife Refuge System and reforested more than 80,000 acres with more than 22 million trees, sequestering 30 million metric tons of carbon over the project's 70-year lifetime.

PETE JEROME, *Refuges and Wildlife Area Supervisor, Southeast Region, Atlanta, GA*

---

i **Uncertainty** is an expression of the degree to which a value (e.g., the future state of the climate system) is unknown. Uncertainty can result from lack of information or from disagreement about what is known or even knowable. It may have many types of sources, from quantifiable errors in the data to ambiguously defined concepts or terminology or uncertain projections of human behavior. Uncertainty can, therefore, be represented by quantitative measures or by qualitative statements.

Scope and Magnitude Are Great

Another major challenge of accelerated climate change is its unprecedented scope and magnitude. In the history of wildlife conservation, the Service and the larger conservation community have never experienced a challenge that is so ubiquitous across the landscape. Our existing conservation infrastructure will be pressed to its limits—quite likely beyond its limits—to respond successfully. New and different capacities and capabilities will be required, and our dedicated employees will be challenged to acquire new skills quickly. We may find that elements of our current legal, regulatory, and policy frameworks within which we and our partners operate are no longer adequate to encourage and support the new approaches and innovative thinking needed to address climate change effectively. In our land management, the original purposes for which some of our National Wildlife Refuges have been established may change or become obsolete. We will need financial and technological resources commensurate with this great challenge; and we will need the political leadership and will to pursue necessary statutory and regulatory changes, apply predictive models, make risk-based decisions, and manage and operate adaptively in changing environments.

Making people more aware of how accelerating climate change is harming fish and wildlife and of how it reduces the flow of societal goods and affects ecosystem services is a challenge for the Service, our State and Tribal counterparts, and the conservation community at large. The same ecosystem functions that provide for sustainable fish and wildlife populations also provide communities with significant benefits, such as good water quality, flood and fire protection, and recreation. Meeting the challenge will require that the Service and its partners use every available communication tool to engage the public about the ecological, economic, social, and cultural costs exacted by climate change.

> *The same ecosystem functions that provide for sustainable fish and wildlife populations also provide communities with significant benefits, such as good water quality, flood and fire protection, and recreation.*

Determining Effects of Climate Change on Rio Grande Cutthroat Trout

Air temperature in the Southwest has increased markedly over the last 30 years, and greater increases are predicted. Because air temperature strongly influences water temperature, the temperature of streams that harbor our native Rio Grande cutthroat trout may have already increased, or likely will increase. Trout love cold water. Warmer water temperatures could affect their health, their ability to compete with non-native trout, the amount of suitable habitat available to them, and their food supply. The Service's Southwest Region is funding research to examine historical water temperatures in comparison to current water temperatures in streams occupied by Rio Grande cutthroat trout. In conjunction with other studies that look at the temperature tolerance of Rio Grande cutthroat trout, this research will help us determine the level of risk that increased water temperatures pose to this species.

MARILYN MYERS, *Lead Biologist for Rio Grande cutthroat trout, Ecological Services Field Office, Albuquerque, NM*

(Above) Rio Grande cutthroat trout caught during population sampling on the Rio Santa Barbara in New Mexico. Photo: Yvette Paroz / New Mexico Department of Game and Fish

Our Committed Response

IN OUR STRATEGIC PLAN, WE COMMIT TO CREATING AN INFORMED, CREDIBLE CLIMATE CHANGE LEADERSHIP and management capability that will implement the plan in a collaborative and scientifically sound manner. We will take bold actions, expressed as Seven Bold Commitments, that we believe will help to shape the conservation community's response to the impacts of this global environmental scourge on fish, wildlife and habitats. We will employ three progressive strategies—Adaptation, Mitigation, and Engagement — in carrying out our strategic goals and objectives. Through this cohesive, integrated response, we will fulfill our commitment to the American people and take our appropriate role within the conservation community in addressing the challenges presented by accelerating climate change.

Leadership and Management

We anticipate that within the next few years, the U.S. Congress and the Federal Government will make political decisions and policies relative to climate change that will have enormous significance for 21st century conservation of fish and wildlife and their habitats. To help shape these decisions and policies, the Service must already have in place at the national and regional levels a climate change leadership and management capability that can provide a credible and cohesive approach to the issue. Our National Climate Team and eight Regional Climate Teams, operating under the guidance of our Directorate and its National Science Applications Executive Team, will help us establish that capability and credibility.

The National Climate Team will have representation from Service regions and programs; and the Regional Climate Teams will be made up of both Regional Office and field employees. Together, these teams will provide input to the development of national climate change policies and guidance; and provide leadership and direction in the management of the Service's climate change activities, including budget and performance; policy development and implementation; landscape conservation design, delivery, and evaluation; internal and external partnership development; Congressional assistance; engagement and communication; and science direction.

Accomplishing our mission in an era of accelerated climate change will require a fundamental rethinking of how we in the Service do business in the coming decades, including how we define leaders and leadership and how we manage and deliver our conservation activities.

The exercise of leadership will not be limited to the Directorate or the National and Regional Climate Teams; it must permeate all levels of the Service. The crisis of a changing climate is unlike any other we have faced in world history. Climate change is not the result of the actions of the few that are impacting the many; it is the direct result of the activities of each one of us as we live and work in the modern world. In a crisis of this magnitude and scope, we must each take leadership in our own sphere of influence to make the changes that will eliminate or reduce the causative factors of climate change. As Service employees, we each have the added responsibility of taking leadership within our professional spheres of influence to address the impacts that climate change is already having or will have on fish, wildlife and habitats.

The Directorate and the Washington Office must lead the way by recognizing the crisis nature of climate change and seeking the resources needed to address it; by making difficult choices about Service program priorities and budgets that will guide and define our activities; and by calling upon every employee to get appropriately involved in our adaptation, mitigation, and engagement strategies.

Regional leaders and employees must lead the way by stepping down national guidance and plans to the field, facilitating the feedback loop between national leadership and the field, ensuring that resources to accomplish work on the ground reach those who need them, and removing any barriers to success.

Project leaders and field employees must lead the way by ground-truthing our efforts, implementing our strategies, monitoring our results, and recommending new approaches as necessary.

All employees must lead the way by participating in the creation of new climate change partnerships, and by working with others to find new and innovative means for incorporating climate change considerations into our day-to-day activities.

Climate change leadership will function in much the same way as our Strategic Habitat Conservation approach— it will be more iterative than hierarchical, with Service leaders at each level making indispensable and ongoing contributions as they operate in constellation with one another.

Our Committed Response

Climate Change Entrepreneurs

As a Service, we will approach the management and delivery of our conservation activities with a new spirit of entrepreneurship, which we define as "the process of identifying, evaluating, and seizing an opportunity and bringing together the resources necessary for success." As climate change entrepreneurs, we will learn and embrace new conservation approaches that lead to better results for fish and wildlife. We will face hard facts, and we will redirect our priorities and make difficult budget decisions as those facts dictate. We will hold ourselves accountable, formally monitoring and evaluating the effectiveness of our efforts as we implement our Strategic Plan and our 5-Year Action Plan. We will seek outside, independent reviews of our climate change efforts after 3 years. We will recognize and reward Service employees, programs, or offices that demonstrate entrepreneurship by taking substantive actions on climate change adaptation, mitigation, or engagement.

Leading Through Action

As a Service, we willingly accept the opportunity to be a leader on climate change within the fish and wildlife conservation community, recognizing that this leadership will be demonstrated through actions, not words. We will show leadership by working with States, Tribes, and others to effectively represent fish and wildlife conservation interests in discussions relating to national climate policy and legislation. We will also work with the conservation community to help create climate change legislation that incorporates wildlife adaptation strategies, as outlined in our

Climate Change Implicated in the Mystery of the Dying Moose

No visit to northern Minnesota is complete without seeing a moose. So you can imagine our concern here at Agassiz National Wildlife Refuge when the moose population dropped dramatically in a few years' time. The Refuge was once home to 250 to 400 moose. Today, it is estimated that less than 40 remain on Agassiz. The decline in population on the Refuge was part of a regional decline in Northwest Minnesota.

This population fell from a peak of 4,000 animals in 1984 to a low of about 85 in 2007. A research study initiated in 1985 with the Minnesota Department of Natural Resources and support from citizens, landowners, and volunteers concluded that climatic changes, combined with increased deer numbers and parasitic transmission rates, may have rendered Northwest Minnesota inhospitable to moose. Winter and summer temperatures in the past 41 years have increased by about 12°F and 4°F, respectively. The study showed that moose declines often occurred the year after summers with higher mean temperatures. Moose have temperature thresholds that, when exceeded, require them to expend energy to keep cool. The data indicates that warmer temperatures may have contributed to heat stress, which in turn accentuated the animals' already poor body condition from parasite-induced chronic malnutrition. The bottom line: Until the climatic factors that are making the moose range shrink are reversed, we will probably see fewer moose in Northwest Minnesota.

MAGGIE ANDERSON, *Manager, Agassiz National Wildlife Refuge, Middle River, MN*

(Above) Bull moose. Photo: Beth Silverhus

Strategic Plan, and that reflects our climate change principles for addressing this conservation challenge. We will play a key role in galvanizing governments, organizations, businesses and industry to collaborate in developing a National Fish and Wildlife Climate Adaptation Strategy and partnering in its implementation.

Conservation Through Collaboration

As a conservation leader, the Service recognizes that the crisis of climate change also opens up great opportunities for those of us committed to the sustainability of our nation's fish and wildlife resources. This crisis is an opportunity to expand and strengthen our partnerships in ways that will inevitably help us to more effectively address not just this threat to the future of fish and wildlife but all other threats, such as unsustainable land-use practices, degradation of water quality and quantity, and invasive species. It is an opportunity to for us to "take it to the next level" scientifically by building an unequalled network of shared scientific capacity, capability and knowledge that we can draw upon in every decision we make. It is an opportunity to engage the public as never before in facing the fact that our actions, individually and collectively, have implications for the future of fish, wildlife, people, and the planet. The crisis of climate change is, in the final analysis, an unparalleled opportunity to bring people together, nationally and internationally, to solve a world problem, not through conflict but through collaboration.

We acknowledge that this Strategic Plan and its accompanying 5-Year Action Plan call upon Service employees to engage in many new teams, partnerships, and assessments. We take as a given that it is the responsibility of leadership at each level in the Service to pursue and make available to employees the resources, time, training, and tools to accomplish our mission. It is worth noting that climate change is not a new mission; it is the lens through which we must accomplish the mission we already have. As we address climate change in carrying out that mission, we will seek

Climate change is not a new mission; it is the lens through which we must accomplish the mission we already have.

new resources that we need, reprioritize and reallocate the resources we have, and leverage our collective resources by working in partnerships, internally and externally. Our greatest certainty of receiving additional resources is to demonstrate leadership on climate change by assembling our best talent and aligning our present resources and priorities in response to this challenge. Our nation is at a turning point in regard to climate change, and we have the opportunity and the responsibility to help tip the balance in favor of aggressive action.

Given the magnitude of the threat posed by climate change to life as we know it, we cannot afford to think small or be held back by our fears or concerns. All great achievements in human history have occurred within the context of daunting challenges and have been accomplished by people with vision who were willing to move forward without having all the answers and resources they would have desired. Our National Wildlife Refuge System, a 150-million-acre network of lands and waters spread from "sea to shining sea," is a sterling example of what can happen when even one person with courage and vision is willing to stand in the breach for wildlife and call the nation's attention to the threat at hand. This is our moment, as individuals and as a Service, to rise to the threat posed by climate change. If we succeed, we will have done our duty. If we fail, it will not be said of us that we were afraid to try.

Seven Bold Commitments

We will fulfill our leadership role as the principal national agency through which the Federal Government carries out its fish, wildlife, and habitat conservation mission for the American public by committing to seven bold undertakings that we believe are essential to our success in effectively responding to the threats posed by climate change. As a Service, we will:

1. Establish new, shared scientific and technical capacity within the conservation community in the form of **Regional Climate Science Partnerships** to acquire and translate climate change information into knowledge that together we can apply to better predict, understand and address the effects of climate change on fish, wildlife and their habitats at all spatial scales.

2. Establish **Landscape Conservation Cooperatives** that enable members of the conservation community to plan, design and deliver conservation in ways that integrate local, State, Tribal, regional, national and international efforts and resources, with our 150 million-acre National Wildlife Refuge System playing a role in ensuring habitat connectivity and conserving key landscapes and populations of fish and wildlife.

3. Develop new organizational and managerial processes and procedures that enable the Service to evaluate its actions, decisions, and expenditures through the lens of climate change and that unite us across our programs in a shared commitment to address the effects of climate change on fish and wildlife and their habitats.

4. Use our informational, educational, training, and outreach capabilities to engage our employees, our conservation partners, business and industry, government and non-government organizations, the public, and other internal and external audiences in a dialogue about the consequences of climate change; and inspire their innovative actions to combat its effects on fish, wildlife, habitats, and people.

5. Become carbon neutral as an agency by Year 2020 and encourage other organizations to do the same.

6. Apply Strategic Habitat Conservation[8] as the Service's framework for landscape conservation.

7. Inspire and lead the conservation community in creating and implementing a shared national vision for addressing climate change by:

• Facilitating development of a **National Fish and Wildlife Climate Adaptation Strategy** that would be our shared blueprint to guide wildlife adaptation partnerships over the next 50–100 years;

• Creating a **National Biological Inventory and Monitoring Partnership** that facilitates a more strategic and cohesive use of the conservation community's monitoring resources. The Partnership would generate empirical data needed to track climate change effects on the distribution and abundance of fish, wildlife and their habitats; model predicted population and habitat change; and help us determine if we are achieving our goals;

• Organizing a **National Climate Change Forum** where members of the conservation community can exchange ideas and knowledge, network, and build the relationships that will ensure our success in addressing climate change.

Three Progressive Strategies: Adaptation, Mitigation, Engagement

Our Strategic Plan's goals, objectives, and actions are positioned under three major strategies that correspond with the Service's mission. These strategies are:

Adaptation: Minimizing the impact of climate change on fish and wildlife through the application of cutting-edge science in managing species and habitats.

Mitigation: Reducing levels of greenhouse gases in the Earth's atmosphere.

Engagement: Joining forces with others to seek solutions to the challenges and threats to fish and wildlife conservation posed by climate change.

Vision without action is merely a dream. Action without vision just passes the time. Vision with action can change the world.

JOEL BARKER, living American scholar and futurist who was the first to popularize the concept of paradigm shifts in the corporate world

---

Adaptation

Adaptation is defined by the IPCC as "an adjustment in natural or human systems in response to actual or expected climatic stimuli or their effects, which moderates harm or exploits beneficial opportunities." For the Service, adaptation is planned, science-based management actions, including regulatory and policy changes, that we take to help reduce the impacts of climate change on fish, wildlife, and their habitats. Adaptation forms the core of the Service's response to climate change and is the centerpiece of our Strategic Plan.

Our principal approach to fish and wildlife adaptation will involve the strategic conservation of terrestrial, freshwater, and marine habitats within sustainable landscapes to achieve the fundamental goal of conserving target populations of species or suites of species and the ecological functions that sustain them. We have termed this strategic approach to achieving our landscape conservation objectives Strategic Habitat Conservation, or SHC.

SHC is an explicit, adaptive approach to conservation. It takes as a given that effective conservation always necessitates that we answer a few basic questions and that the same is true for SHC: First, what are our goals? What healthy populations of species do we seek to conserve, and what specifically are our targets? Second, how can we develop a conservation design to meet these goals? Third, how will we deliver this conservation approach? Fourth, what sorts of monitoring will be needed to determine whether we've been successful or whether we need to adapt our strategies? Fifth, what new scientific research do we need to meet our conservation objectives?

These ideas are not new; they are key components of any adaptive management or landscape-scale conservation strategy. Distilled, they are the five elements of Strategic Habitat Conservation:

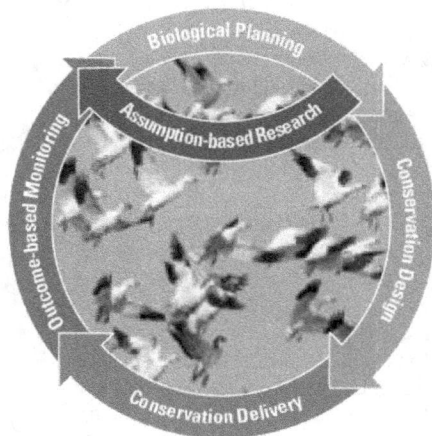

Element 1: *Biological Planning*: Set targets/goals

Element 2: *Conservation Design*: Develop a plan to meet the targets/goals

Element 3: *Conservation Delivery*: Implement the plan

Element 4: *Outcome-based Monitoring and Adaptive Management*: Measure success and improve results

Element 5: *Assumption-Based Research*: Increase knowledge and understanding through iteration (repetitive looping) of all five elements in conjunction with one another.

In adopting the SHC framework to address climate change impacts, the Service acknowledges that it needs a structured, objective-driven process for biological planning and conservation design; predictive models for managed ecosystems, especially models that acknowledge uncertainties and challenge our decisions; monitoring to improve our understanding and management; and effective ways of delivering conservation actions on the ground that will typically require extensive partnerships and collaboration.[9]

The Service recognizes four basic approaches, or strategies, to climate change adaptation for fish and wildlife resources (based on Millar et al. 2007): resistance, resilience, response and realignment.

Resistance

Traditional and current approaches to conservation have been directed primarily toward maintaining current or restoring historic conditions. In many cases, maintaining or restoring these conditions means working *against* the effects of climate change as they occur on the landscape. Resistance adaptation options seek to manage fish and wildlife resources "to resist the influence of climate change or to forestall undesired effects of change."[10] Resistance actions will be most effective when the magnitude of climate change is small; or, when the magnitude is greater, "to save native species and habitats for the short term—perhaps a few decades—until other adaptation options are found."[11] Resisting climate changes may require intensive management action, and accelerating effort and greater investments over time. It also requires recognition that these efforts may fail as cumulative change in conditions may be so substantial that resistance is no longer possible.[10]

Conserving and Managing Apache Trout in a Warmer, Drier Southwest

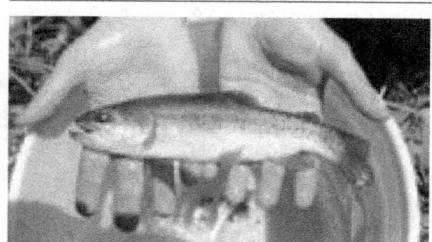

In a region already known for its warm temperatures and relatively low precipitation, aquatic species in the Southwest may be vulnerable due to climate change. What will this mean for the conservation and recovery of Apache trout? Climate models for the Southwest predict a continuing increase in drought and flood severity, warmer air and water temperatures, less precipitation, and more water loss through plant transpiration and ground evaporation, as well as an increase in events such as wildfire and extreme drought. Warming trends may alter seasonal river flows, making them higher during winter and lower during summer. Less snowfall and more rain during winter may result in earlier spring runoff (an important cue for the spring-spawning Apache trout). Post-wildfire flooding can eliminate populations and can make streams uninhabitable for years. We are working with our partners to identify strategies to address these new threats through habitat protection, restoration to increase habitat resiliency, and monitoring. Understanding how climate change may influence habitat for Apache trout will be critical for effective management and recovery of this species.

JEREMY VOELTZ, *Lead Biologist, Apache Trout Recovery Program, Pinetop, AZ*

Apache trout taken from Arizona creek Photo: Jeremy Voeltz / USFWS

Resilience

Resilience is the ability of a natural system to return to a desired condition after disturbance, either naturally or with management assistance. Resilience adaptation options, then, are management actions that improve the capacity of ecosystems to return to desired conditions after disturbance. Fostering resilience is probably the most frequently suggested approach to adaptation found in climate change literature.[10] Management practices that facilitate resilience are similar to those used to resist change (e.g., habitat restoration, habitat management with fire or through invasive removal), but are usually applied more broadly and are specifically aimed at coping with disturbance.[10] Maintaining or improving habitat or ecosystem resilience may become more difficult and require more intensive management as changes in climate accumulate over time.[10] Resilience adaptation does not facilitate the transition to new conditions that are likely to result from climate change.[11] Thus, some authorities indicate that resilience options are best undertaken in projects that are short term or under ecosystem conditions that are relatively insensitive to climate change effects.[10]

Response

Another approach to climate change is to manage toward future, and often less certain, landscape conditions by predicting and working *with* the effects of climate change. Response adaptation options facilitate the transition of ecosystems from current, natural states to new conditions brought about by a changing climate. Response management actions "mimic, assist or enable ongoing natural adaptive processes, such as species dispersal and migration, population mortality and colonization, changes in community/ecosystem composition, and changing disturbance regimes…to encourage gradual adaptation and transition to inevitable change, and thereby avoid rapid threshold or catastrophic conversion that may occur otherwise."[10]

Realignment

Restoration is a frequently recommended management approach for ecosystems already significantly disturbed. When the goal of that restoration is to realign a system to expected future conditions rather than return it to historical conditions, realignment adaptation options are used.[10] According to Choi (2007), a "future-oriented restoration should (1) establish the ecosystems that are able to sustain in the future, not the past, environment; (2) have multiple alternative goals and trajectories for unpredictable endpoints; (3) focus on rehabilitation of ecosystem functions rather than re-composition of species or cosmetics of landscape surface; and (4) acknowledge its identity as a 'value-laden' applied science within an economically and socially acceptable framework."[12]

Adaptation approaches to climate change can be implemented in a reactive manner or an anticipatory manner. The IPCC defines **reactive adaptation** as "adaptation that takes place after impacts of climate change have been observed," whereas **anticipatory adaptation** is "adaptation that takes place before impacts of climate change are observed (also referred to as proactive adaptation)." Historically, climate change adaptation by human societies has been reactive, as is all biological adaptation in an evolutionary sense. As our understanding of climate change and its effects on ecosystems increases and uncertainty decreases, we anticipate implementing increasingly more anticipatory adaptation approaches.

We must be explicit and strategic about which adaptation approach we will take in a given situation because an inappropriate response or a series of inconsistent responses can result in large expenditures of time, energy, and resources with questionable or insufficient outcomes. In some situations, our response to climate change will be to implement resistance adaptation measures, as these measures will be sufficient to maintain desired conditions in the face of ongoing climate change. In other situations, we will first implement resistance and/or resilience adaptation measures to maintain current or historical conditions for as long as possible, and then transition to response adaptation measures as our capacity to predict and manage future conditions grows. In still other situations, our certainty regarding future landscape conditions will be adequate to allow us to proceed immediately with response adaptation. For some degraded ecosystems we will restore current or historical conditions to build and maintain resilience, while for others we will implement realignment measures to move the systems toward anticipated future conditions. Our decisions about which adaptation approaches to use will be based on where we stand as a conservation community in terms of climate change knowledge and understanding, management technologies and techniques, and policy constraints and opportunities. We will practice adaptive management where possible, and we will apply other techniques when circumstances dictate. Over time, we will increase the certainty of our collective understanding and actions in regard to climate change impacts.

Mitigation

Mitigation is defined by the IPCC as "human intervention to reduce the sources or enhance the sinks[j] of greenhouse gases." Mitigation involves reducing our carbon footprint by using less energy, reducing our consumption, and appropriately altering our land-management practices, such as wildlife food production. Our goal is to achieve carbon neutrality as an organization by the Year 2020.

Mitigation is also achieved through biological carbon sequestration, which is basically the process by which CO_2 from the atmosphere is taken up by plants through photosynthesis and stored as carbon in biomass (e.g., tree trunks and roots) or stored as organic carbon in soils. Sequestering carbon in vegetation, such as bottomland hardwood forests, can often restore or improve habitat and directly benefit fish and wildlife.

We will be aggressive in sequestering carbon and using best practices to manage our lands, meet our stewardship responsibilities, and manage our facilities, vehicles and vessels, travel, and purchases and acquisitions so that we become carbon neutral by 2020. Our success in pursuing and achieving carbon neutrality will help us to model appropriate organizational behaviors and to participate with the conservation community in catalyzing action to reduce greenhouse gas emissions worldwide. In addition, we expect our mitigation successes to influence local, regional, national, and international land-use and energy policies and actions and to further reduce greenhouse gas emissions, thereby reducing the impacts of climate change on fish, wildlife, and their habitats.

Engagement

Engagement is reaching out to Service employees; our local, national and international partners in the public and private sectors; our key constituencies and stakeholders; and everyday citizens to join forces with them in seeking solutions to the challenges and threats to fish and wildlife conservation posed by climate change. By building knowledge and sharing information in a comprehensive and integrated way, the Service and our partners and stakeholders will increase our understanding of global climate change impacts and use our combined expertise and creativity to help wildlife resources adapt in a climate-changed world. Through engagement, Service employees will be better equipped to address climate change in their day-to-day responsibilities; America's citizens will be inspired to participate in a new era of collaborative environmental stewardship, working to reduce their carbon footprints and supporting wildlife adaptation efforts; and leaders at the local, regional, national, and international levels will be motivated to craft and support legislation and policy that address climate change and consider its impacts to fish and wildlife.

Climate Change and SHC's Five Elements

Climate change is integrally tied to each of SHC's five elements. For example, setting realistic and achievable biological targets requires careful consideration of the effects of climate change; otherwise, we could unwittingly set species goals that rely on locations that won't be available as habitat in the future. The impacts from sea level rise provide a clear example: We anticipate that some of today's valuable coastal habitat will be inundated in the years ahead and, thus, unable to support certain wildlife species. The task before us is to anticipate these changes and incorporate them into our goal-setting, as well as our conservation planning and delivery. We must ask ourselves such fundamental questions as, "Are we conserving the right places based on the changes we anticipate from climate change?"

Climate change also makes monitoring and adaptive management more important than ever. The predicted impacts from climate change are wide-ranging and their timing is highly uncertain. We need monitoring to understand the rate and magnitude of climate change; but more importantly, we need monitoring to understand the effectiveness of our strategies in the face of climate change and other threats. Only then will we be able to effectively modify our strategies over time.

Climate change also must be squarely factored into our research efforts. We must challenge ourselves to envision a future environmental baseline that takes into account the changes in the landscape caused by climate change and other ecosystem change-drivers, such as land use practices. Integrating climate change into our research priorities will help us to create conservation strategies that stand the test of time.

PAUL SOUZA, *Field Supervisor, South Florida Ecological Services Field Office, Vero Beach, FL*

---

j **Sinks** are the removal or sequestration of greenhouse gases.

Our Committed Response

Adaptation, Mitigation, Engagement: A Balanced Approach

We will use a progressive, balanced approach in undertaking adaptation, mitigation and engagement. Goals and objectives in this plan will be stepped down to specific actions that will form our near-term, 5-Year Action Plan for addressing climate change. We will progress in a manner that will reflect increasing certainty[k] about what actions we should take and when we should take them.

We will increase our adaptation efforts significantly in the near term as we respond to increasing climate change impacts. Our initial emphasis will likely be on resistance and resilience types of adaptation, as we work to build resilience in ecosystems through our management efforts and, in some cases, to buy additional time to increase our certainty regarding future landscape conditions. Over the long term, however, we will work with partners to assemble the technical and institutional capability to increase our response and realignment types of adaptation, particularly as we become better able to anticipate the impacts of climate change. As our expertise and that of our conservation partners grows, and as we learn more about climate change, we will increasingly emphasize anticipatory adaptation.

With regard to mitigation, we will begin immediately and work aggressively to reduce our carbon footprint to achieve carbon neutrality. Over time, we anticipate that we will build a strong mitigation consciousness and track record in our organization; consequently, our mitigation efforts will plateau and will be maintained at that level for the long term.

With regard to engagement, we will increase our internal efforts immediately so that our employees can acquire the additional knowledge and skills they need to address climate change as a central focus of our programs and activities. At the same time, we will increase our external engagement to learn from others and help build public support nationally and internationally for the Service's adaptation and mitigation activities. In addition, we will encourage members of the public to join us in reducing their carbon footprints.

...the Service and our partners and stakeholders will increase our understanding of global climate change impacts and use our combined expertise and creativity to help wildlife resources adapt in a climate-changed world.

MINETTE LAYNE / FLICKR

Global climate change may be disrupting migration patterns of species such as hummingbirds that depend on seasonal cues for their survival.

---

k **Certainty** increases when the collective understanding of climate change trajectories in a given area, their impacts on fish and wildlife, and our ability to successfully manage those impacts increases and becomes more accepted, both within the Service and the general public. Increasing certainty within the Service and among our publics and partners is a strategic goal of our research and monitoring programs and our educational endeavors.

Strategic Goals & Objectives

GOALS AND OBJECTIVES WILL TURN OUR STRATEGIC VISION INTO ACTION and position the Service as a responsible leader and creative partner in facilitating wildlife adaptation, greenhouse gas mitigation, and engagement with others to address the effects of accelerating climate change on fish and wildlife and their habitats. Action items needed to achieve these goals and objectives are included in the appendix document, the 5-Year Action Plan.

Adaptation

GOAL 1

We will work with partners to develop and implement a National Fish and Wildlife Climate Adaptation Strategy.

OBJECTIVE 1.1: Inspire, Organize, and Carry Out a Collaborative Process that Brings Together Diverse Interests To Develop a National Fish and Wildlife Climate Adaptation Strategy; and Fully Integrate Resource Management Agencies and Organizations from Around the Country and Internationally into the Process.

Climate legislation proposed in recent sessions of Congress includes provisions for a national strategy for fish and wildlife adaptation to climate change. We view this strategy as the most consequential and crucial conservation endeavor of the 21st century. The Department of the Interior, with the Service as lead agency, and the Council on Environmental Quality are leading the effort to develop a National Fish and Wildlife Climate Adaptation Strategy. We are committed to an intensive, 3-year collaboration with Federal, State, Tribal, and local governments, private landowners, conservation organizations, and international governments and organizations to develop the strategy. The goal is to have a completed strategy by the end of 2012, with implementation to begin soon thereafter. A National Fish and Wildlife Climate Adaptation Strategy is likely to consist of an agreement that identifies and defines integrated approaches to maintaining key terrestrial, freshwater and marine ecosystems and functions needed to sustain fish and wildlife resources in the face of accelerating climate change. As the strategy is developed and implemented, we will work to ensure that it:

(1) embraces the philosophy that maintaining healthy fish and wildlife populations and ecosystem sustainability are interdependent goals;

(2) adopts landscape-scale approaches that integrate science and management;

(3) recognizes appropriate roles for all four adaptation approaches (resistance, resilience, response, realignment);

(4) reflects the uncertainty associated with adaptation planning, but also acknowledges that, over time, we will be better able to be anticipatory and proactive in our approach to adaptation;

(5) addresses species and habitat priorities that are based on scientific assessments and risk-based predictions of vulnerability to changing climate;

(6) considers adaptation strategies being developed for other sectors (such as agriculture, human health and transportation) so that the strategies complement one another and minimize conflicts; and

(7) identifies key ecological processes and methods to conserve priority species and habitats.

For the implementation of landscape-scale conservation, the strategy will place particular emphasis on ecological systems and function; strengthened observational systems; model-based projections; species-habitat linkages; risk assessment; and active and passive adaptive management. The strategy will include a national strategy for monitoring species and habitats that are most vulnerable to climate change. It will also outline appropriate scientific support (including inventory, monitoring, research, and modeling) to inform management decisions; the need for and importance of collaboration and interdependency; and the financial resources (including grants, appropriated funds, and private contributions) needed to implement decisions.

A National Fish and Wildlife Climate Adaptation Strategy will cover the length and breadth of the United States, from the Pacific Islands to the eastern seaboard and from Alaska to the Caribbean; and will extend beyond our borders to encompass habitats used by cross-border species (e.g., those shared with Canada and Mexico)[l], as well as areas in the Western Hemisphere associated with many migratory species (e.g., Central and South American wintering areas of migratory songbirds)[m].

---

l **Trans-boundary issues** will be addressed through the Canada/Mexico/U.S. Trilateral Committee for Wildlife and Ecosystem Conservation and Management (the Trilateral Committee). The Trilateral Committee was established to facilitate and enhance coordination, cooperation, and the development of partnerships among the wildlife agencies of the three countries regarding programs and projects for the conservation and management of species and ecosystems of mutual interest in North America.

m **Western hemisphere migratory species issues** will largely be addressed through the Western Hemisphere Migratory Species Initiative, which seeks to contribute significantly to the conservation of the migratory species of the hemisphere by strengthening communication and cooperation among nations, international conventions, and civil society; and by expanding constituencies and political support.

In short, a National Fish and Wildlife Adaptation Strategy will be our shared blueprint to guide wildlife adaptation partnerships over the next 50–100 years. The strategy will enable the national and international conservation communities to harness collective expertise, authorities, and abilities to define and prioritize a shared set of conservation goals and objectives, as well as to prescribe a plan of integrated, concerted action.

GOAL 2

We will develop long-term capacity for biological planning and conservation design and apply it to drive conservation at broad, landscape scales.

OBJECTIVE 2.1: Access Regional Climate Science and Modeling Expertise through Regional Climate Science Partnerships

Successful conservation strategies will require an understanding of climate change, the ability to predict how that change will affect fish and wildlife at multiple scales, and the skill to translate this understanding into useful tools for landscape-level conservation design. We need access to experts in climate science and modeling who have the capability of putting climate data and projections into forms that are useful for biological planning and conservation design. This expertise can be found within such organizations as the U.S. Geological Survey, the National Oceanic and Atmospheric Administration, universities, and some non-governmental organizations. Because these experts tend to be widely dispersed across the government, conservation, and academic communities, a mechanism is needed that will allow them to effectively collaborate with one another on a regional basis, e.g., through virtual networks. The U.S. Geological Survey is well positioned to coordinate such Regional Climate Science Partnerships through its Climate Change and Wildlife Science Center and the Departmental Climate Science Centers that are being established pursuant to Secretarial Order 3289. We will help the U.S. Geological Survey and the Department with the development of these Regional Climate Science Partnerships to support a broad spectrum of natural resource management activities.

Climate science and modeling expertise will:

(1) make global climate model outputs usable at multiple planning scales through downscaling approaches (either dynamical or statistical);

(2) integrate global or downscaled climate model outputs with ecological and land-use change models to project future changes in the distribution and abundance of fish and wildlife resulting from climate and land-use changes;

(3) identify and predict climate change thresholds for key species and habitats;

(4) facilitate research to address key uncertainties in applying climate change science to fish and wildlife conservation; and

(5) support regional or local climate monitoring programs. Currently, this expertise is not readily available to managers. Without it, they cannot develop successful adaptation strategies for fish and wildlife.

OBJECTIVE 2.2: Develop Landscape Conservation Cooperatives to Acquire Biological Planning and Conservation Design Expertise

To promote wildlife adaptation to accelerating climate change, we need the capability to develop, test, implement, and monitor conservation strategies that will be responsive to the dynamic landscape changes resulting from climate change. These strategies must be model-based and spatially explicit, allowing us to effectively apply our emerging climate knowledge to predict habitat and species changes and to design our conservation actions to target impacts. To accomplish this, we will develop biological planning, conservation design, and research and monitoring expertise across the Service and among diverse partners, as defined in our Strategic Habitat Conservation framework.

We will work interdependently with partners to develop this expertise within Landscape Conservation Cooperatives (LCCs). LCCs are formal partnerships between Federal and State agencies, Tribes, non-government organizations, universities and others to share conservation science capacity (including staff) to address landscape-scale stressors, including habitat fragmentation, genetic isolation, spread of invasive species, and water scarcity, all of which are accelerated by climate change. LCCs are envisioned as the centerpiece of the Service's and the Department's (via Secretarial Order 3289) informed management response to climate change impacts on natural resources.

The precise organizational structure for LCCs will vary based on the shared needs of cooperators. Rather than create a new conservation infrastructure from the ground up, LCCs will build upon the science and the management priorities of existing partnerships, such as fish habitat partnerships, migratory bird joint ventures and flyway councils, as well as species- and geographic-based partnerships. All LCCs will be guided by a steering committee composed of representatives of partner organizations, and all will be focused on defined geographic areas. The Service has developed an Interim Geographic Framework that will form the basis for the nationwide network of LCCs. Ultimately, 21 LCCs will be established.

With the expertise available through LCCs, we and our partners will assemble climate, land-cover, land-use, hydrological and other relevant data in spatially explicit contexts to develop explicit, predictive and measurable biological objectives to guide landscape-scale conservation design. We will use results from population-habitat and ecological models, statistical analyses, and geographic information systems to design conservation strategies that drive conservation delivery at landscape scales. We will develop scientifically valid, collaborative population and habitat monitoring programs that are linked to and support agency decision-making processes. We will develop and facilitate research projects focused explicitly on the documented assumptions and uncertainties resulting from biological planning and conservation design activities.

OBJECTIVE 2.3: Develop Expertise In and Conduct Adaptation Planning for Key Species and Habitats

Adaptation planning will fall within the purview of LCCs, as well as individual Service programs. In addition to those generally used in SHC, new tools will be required for development of successful climate change adaptation plans. These tools will include species and habitat vulnerability assessments; planning and decision-support tools, such as scenario planning; the use of high-resolution climate projections to drive important ecological and biophysical response models; risk assessments; and green infrastructure planning. To facilitate adaptation planning within and across LCCs, we will assemble available information and provide

Interim Geographic Framework for Landscape Conservation Cooperatives

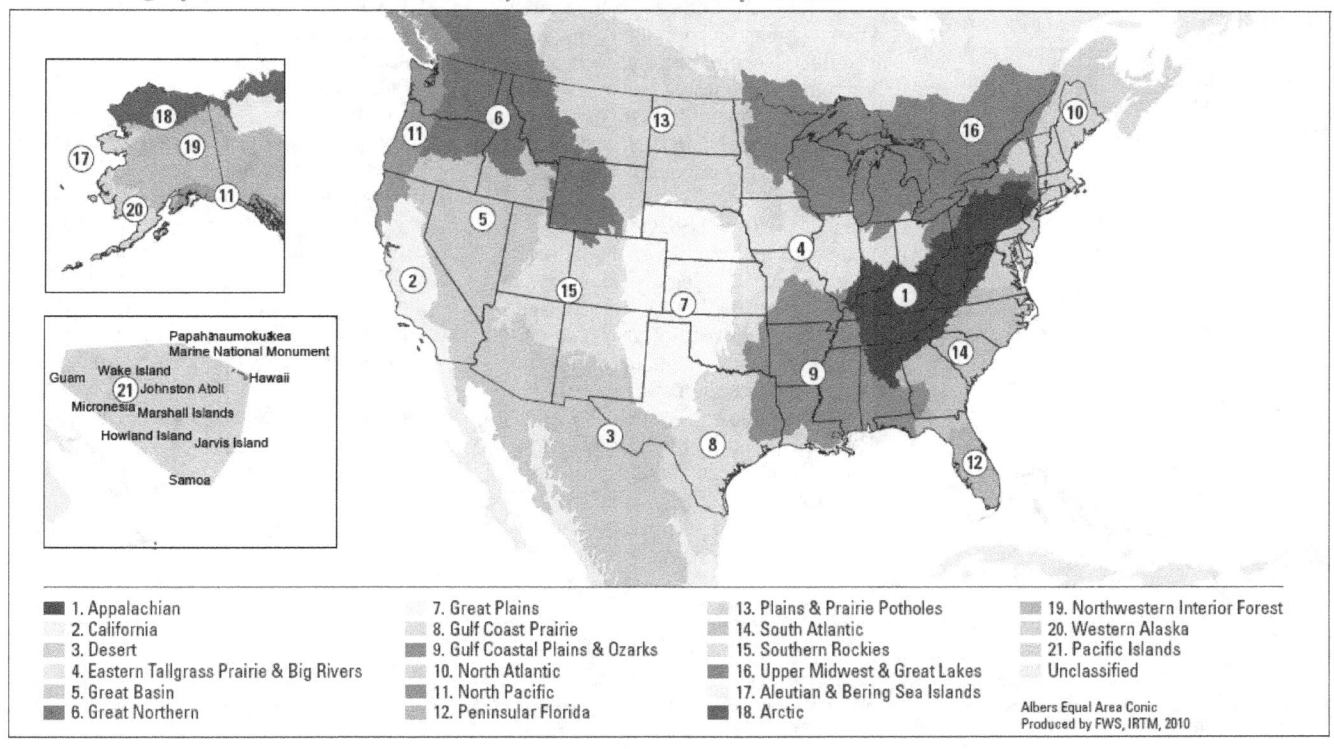

1. Appalachian	7. Great Plains	13. Plains & Prairie Potholes	19. Northwestern Interior Forest
2. California	8. Gulf Coast Prairie	14. South Atlantic	20. Western Alaska
3. Desert	9. Gulf Coastal Plains & Ozarks	15. Southern Rockies	21. Pacific Islands
4. Eastern Tallgrass Prairie & Big Rivers	10. North Atlantic	16. Upper Midwest & Great Lakes	Unclassified
5. Great Basin	11. North Pacific	17. Aleutian & Bering Sea Islands	
6. Great Northern	12. Peninsular Florida	18. Arctic	Albers Equal Area Conic Produced by FWS, IRTM, 2010

recommendations on best planning practices. This may involve providing a variety of acceptable options to use in different situations and the pros and cons of each; and it will include identifying any crucial gaps in data, capacity, or training that need to be addressed.

One fundamental step in adaptation planning is determining which species and habitats are most vulnerable to accelerating climate change ("climate-vulnerable"). As previously defined, vulnerability is a function of the sensitivity of a particular system to climate changes, its exposure to those changes, and its capacity to adapt to those changes. We will work with partners and with regional and field staff to develop methodologies to assess species and habitat vulnerability and to test and apply these methodologies on the ground. Climate vulnerability assessments will be used in conjunction with analyses of non-climate stressors (such as water quantity and quality for aquatic species, spread of invasive species, impacts of fire regimes, exposure to contaminants, and changes in land use) to assess the overall vulnerability of species and habitats.

OBJECTIVE 2.4: Incorporate Climate Change in Service Activities and Decisions

We will consider actual and projected climate change impacts to fish and wildlife populations and their habitats in Service planning, decision-making, consultation and evaluation, management, and restoration efforts. Planning efforts will include resource planning (e.g., recovery plans, habitat conservation plans, fish habitat plans, migratory bird plans, natural resource damage restoration plans, and Comprehensive Conservation Plans); operations planning (e.g., facility maintenance, construction, and equipment and fleet management); and administrative planning (e.g., workforce planning, and information technology management planning). Decision-making includes Endangered Species Act listing decisions and injurious wildlife listing decisions. Consultation and evaluation includes Endangered Species Act Section 7 consultations and related documents, such as biological opinions, Fish and Wildlife Coordination Act evaluations, and environmental assessments. We will prepare guidance that can be used by our various programs in their assessment of climate change impacts.

We will review all Service grant programs and modify grant criteria, as necessary and legally allowable, to direct more funding to projects that specifically address climate change adaptation, mitigation, or engagement. Where modification of grant criteria is not legally allowable, such as Pittman-Robertson and Dingell-Johnson grants made through the Wildlife and Sport Fish Restoration programs, we will work with partners to encourage grantees to consider climate change initiatives.

OBJECTIVE 2.5: Provide Requested Support to State and Tribal Managers to Address Climate Change Issues that Affect Fish and Wildlife Service Trust Resources

Many States are already working to address climate change in their State Wildlife Action Plans and other management plans, and Tribes are likely to undertake similar measures in their resource management plans. When requested, we will work collaboratively with States and Tribes to share information and to support their efforts to incorporate climate change considerations into their fish and wildlife management plans and programs.

OBJECTIVE 2.6: Evaluate Fish and Wildlife Service Laws, Regulations, and Policies to Identify Barriers To and Opportunities for Successful Implementation of Climate Change Actions

We will review the Service's laws, regulations, and policies to determine what, if any, changes may be necessary to support effective adaptation and mitigation responses to climate change. We will focus particularly on determining the need to develop new policies (e.g., for managed relocation[n]) and necessary revisions of existing policies (e.g., what constitutes native, invasive, or exotic species). In addition, we will identify new (or revisions to) laws, regulations, policies, guidance, and other protocols necessary to provide incentives or eliminate barriers to our efforts to mitigate climate change by reducing our carbon footprint.

n **Managed relocation** is the intentional translocation of a species with limited dispersal ability to a site or sites where it currently does not occur or has not been known to occur in recent history and where the probability of persistence in the face of climate change is predicted to be higher.

GOAL 3

We will plan and deliver landscape conservation actions that support climate change adaptations by fish and wildlife of ecological and societal significance.

Our long-term approach to climate change will be guided by a National Fish and Wildlife Climate Adaptation Strategy, a coordinated, multi-organization plan for landscape conservation across the United States, portions of Mexico and Canada, and certain, more distant areas within Central and South America.

We anticipate that a strategy will be completed by the end of 2012. In the meantime, there are many on-the-ground efforts we can take with our partners to begin the process of facilitating fish and wildlife adaptation to climate change. As we implement these near-term efforts, we will evaluate success and failure and use this information to inform development and implementation of the national strategy.

OBJECTIVE 3.1: Take Conservation Action for Climate-Vulnerable Species

We will rely on results of our vulnerability assessments and on our field expertise in focusing our efforts to protect species that are particularly vulnerable to climate change, such as sea ice-dependent or sky island[o] animal species and a number of rare and/or endemic plant species. Timely identification of climate-vulnerable species and habitats is critical, as it will allow us to design and implement proactive conservation measures; help us to make decisions regarding listing

species and designation or revision of critical habitat under the Endangered Species Act; help us to revise recovery efforts for already-listed species; and help us to revise various species-related conservation plans, such as the North American Waterbird Conservation Plan. LCCs will be largely responsible for identifying priority species through vulnerability assessments; but other programs, such as Endangered Species and Migratory Birds, will also be involved through their program activities. For example, the Migratory Birds Program was instrumental in producing *The State of the Birds: 2010 Report on Climate Change*, which has helped focus attention on climate-vulnerable bird species.

OBJECTIVE 3.2: Promote Habitat Connectivity and Integrity

Climate change is contributing to the loss, degradation, and fragmentation of current habitats and will likely create novel habitats as species redistribute themselves across the landscape. In addition, climate change is interacting with non-climate stressors — such as land-use change, wildfire, urban and suburban development, and agriculture — to fragment habitats at ever-increasing rates. Protecting and restoring contiguous blocks of unfragmented habitat; and using linkages and corridors to enhance connectivity between habitat blocks (in particular, protected areas such as National Wildlife Refuges) will likely facilitate the movement of fish and wildlife species responding to climate change. Novel conservation measures that address the dynamic nature of climate change effects on habitat may also be needed[13], among them, long-term climate refugia; protected habitat areas with dynamic

boundaries; or other conservation entities, such as land facets[p 14]. Through conservation designs developed by LCCs, we will work with partners to identify needed habitat protection and landscape-scale habitat linkages and corridors. By joining the habitat protection and management capacities of the Service (e.g., National Wildlife Refuge System, Partners for Fish and Wildlife Program, Endangered Species Program, National Fish Habitat Plan, National Fish Passage Program, Neotropical Migratory Bird Conservation Act, and North American Wetlands Conservation Act) with those of our partners, we will help build this connectivity within and between landscapes.

We must also strive to maintain ecosystem integrity and resilience by developing new and innovative ways of protecting and restoring key ecological processes to sustain fish and wildlife. Processes such as pollination, seed dispersal, nutrient cycling, natural disturbance cycles, predator-prey relations, and others must be part of the natural landscapes we seek to maintain or restore. These processes are likely to function more optimally in landscapes composed of large habitat blocks connected by well-placed corridors. We will work with partners to identify how key ecological processes are likely to be affected by climate change, and to determine how management actions might help maintain or restore key ecological processes. We will also conduct research (see Objective 4.4) and create demonstration projects, particularly on Land Management Research and Demonstration areas[q] on National Wildlife Refuges, to evaluate management actions designed to maintain or restore key ecological processes.

---

o **Sky islands** are isolated ecosystems occurring at high elevations (such as on mountain tops) that show evolutionary tendencies similar to those occurring on islands such as the Galapagos Islands.

p **Land facets** are recurring landscape units with uniform topographic and soil attributes.

q **Land Management Research and Demonstration** areas are places on a small number of our National Wildlife Refuges where new habitat management techniques and approaches are developed, implemented and showcased.

OBJECTIVE 3.3: Reduce Non-Climate Change Ecosystem Stressors

Successful adaptation strategies for fish and wildlife will require understanding and reducing the combined and cumulative effects of both climate-related and non-climate stressors. Non-climate stressors include land-use changes (e.g., agricultural conversion, energy development, urbanization); invasive species; unnatural wildfire; contaminants; and wildlife crime. Reducing these non-climate stressors is a fundamental objective of many current Service programs and activities; however, in the face of climate change, it essential that we and our partners be strategic in targeting our efforts where they will do the most good in conserving what we identify as priority species and landscapes. We can no longer afford to simply work to reduce non-climate stressors on an ad hoc or opportunistic basis. Our work must be targeted to reduce specific stressors that our predictive tools indicate will be key limiting factors in an overall adaptation strategy for priority species or landscapes. Reducing these key non-climate stressors will be an important component of the conservation designs for priority landscapes that are developed by LCCs.

OBJECTIVE 3.4: Identify and Fill Priority Freshwater Needs

Water is the key to life, and climate change will alter the distribution, abundance, and quality of water by affecting precipitation, air and water temperatures, and snowmelt. Climate change will drive adaptations of our nation's water supply infrastructure and allocations to meet human needs for water. As these human adaptations are crafted, we will work with partners, including water management agencies, to ensure water resources of adequate quantity and quality to support biological objectives for fish and wildlife are incorporated. This will be a critical issue for our National Wildlife Refuges and National Fish Hatcheries and our conservation efforts for threatened and endangered species, migratory birds, and fish and aquatic species. We will inventory and monitor water quantity and quality, especially relative to National Wildlife Refuges (as described in the Refuge System's draft *Strategic Plan for Inventories and Monitoring on National Wildlife Refuges: Adapting to Environmental Change*). We will work to acquire, manage, and protect adequate supplies of clean water, and to ensure water management authorities provide adequate in-stream flows to address priority needs as determined by vulnerability assessments. We will work to improve water quality, e.g., by reducing environmental contaminant loads or reducing stream temperatures through riparian restoration.

OBJECTIVE 3.5: Conserve Coastal and Marine Resources

Coastal habitats, including estuaries, wetlands (freshwater, brackish, and saline), and beaches, are among the most important habitats for fish and wildlife, including a myriad of migratory bird species and many threatened or endangered species, such as marine turtles and manatees. As such, a large number of our National Wildlife Refuges are along coastlines. Coastal habitats, especially those in the East (particularly mid-Atlantic and Southeast) and the Gulf Coast, are particularly susceptible to sea level rise, as well as to increasing intensity and frequency of storms and storm surges. To begin planning for future management, we must understand the vulnerability of our coastal resources to sea level rise and storms. We will conduct sea level rise modeling (e.g., Sea Level Affecting Marshes Model[r]) for all coastal refuges and expand modeling to additional coastal areas, as practicable, to determine the vulnerability of these areas. We will work with partners to develop new climate-change adaptation strategies for coastal management and restoration. We will implement these strategies as part of landscape conservation designs developed by LCCs. National Wildlife Refuge planners will use the results of vulnerability assessments to design adaptation strategies appropriate for their respective refuges.

Marine ecosystems, especially coral reefs, are among the most biologically diverse ecosystems in the world. Marine resources are threatened by upper-ocean warming, sea-ice retreat, sea level rise, ocean acidification, altered freshwater distributions, and perhaps even strong storms and altered storm tracks, all due to rising levels of atmospheric carbon dioxide and climate change. We must determine the vulnerability to climate change of our marine National Wildlife Refuges, National Monuments, other protected areas, and other priority marine resources as a result of climate change. We will work with partners to develop and implement new climate change adaptation strategies for marine management and restoration.

---

r The **Sea Level Affecting Marshes Model (SLAMM)** simulates the dominant processes involved in wetland conversions and shoreline modifications during long-term sea level rise. Map distributions of wetlands are predicted under conditions of accelerated sea level rise, and results are summarized in tabular and graphical form.

OBJECTIVE 3.6: Manage Genetic Resources

Conservation genetics helps the Service and its partners better measure and assess the taxonomic status and genetic relationships within and among species of fish, wildlife and plants. Genetic variation provides the raw material for species adaptation and evolutionary flexibility in response to environmental change. Maintaining genetic diversity is essential for maintaining healthy, resilient populations of fish, wildlife and plants that are more able to cope with the stressors of climate change. Often as genetic diversity declines, a species' ability to adapt to change decreases and extinction risk increases. Furthermore, when habitat shifts occur, managers can use genetic information to help conserve the genetic diversity anda variability within a species.

We must increase our capacity to gather, interpret, and use genetic information for the conservation of climate-vulnerable species. We will strengthen and expand our genetic analysis and cryopreservation capabilities. We will continue to expand our partnerships with States, zoos, botanical gardens, and other partners to develop other effective ways to manage genetic resources of both captive and wild fish and wildlife populations and to build the policy framework and decision support needed to determine when and how to apply these genetic management measures in a transparent, responsible, and ethical manner.

OBJECTIVE 3.7: Reduce Susceptibility to Diseases, Pathogens, and Pests

Climate-induced stress will compromise species' resistance to diseases and pests and will likely increase mortality. In addition, changing climate will allow pathogens and pests to spread to areas where they are currently limited by climate (e.g., by low temperatures in the winter). Working with our partners and using the existing disease surveillance and diagnostic infrastructure, we will improve surveillance and response capabilities; improve predictions of climate change impacts on the biology of wildlife and vector species; and identify and implement management measures to reduce wildlife vulnerabilities to climate change and susceptibility to disease, pathogens, and pests.

OBJECTIVE 3.8: Address Fish and Wildlife Needs in Renewable Energy Development

As wildlife management professionals, we believe that renewable sources of energy are a key element in mitigating emissions of greenhouse gases, which are the root cause of the climate crisis and its consequences for fish and wildlife. While the expansion of renewable energy development will contribute to the nation's energy needs with lower net atmospheric release of greenhouse gases per unit of energy as compared to nonrenewable sources, we recognize that such development will result in impacts to fish and wildlife. We will facilitate balanced renewable energy development by providing timely and reliable information on impacts to fish and wildlife. We will consider renewable energy project proposals in the context of their expected cumulative impacts to fish and wildlife populations, applying the shared expertise within LCCs; and we will be an objective source of information on how to avoid, minimize, and off-set those effects. We will work with industry, agencies, and other stakeholders to facilitate siting, construction, operation and maintenance of renewable energy projects that explicitly evaluate and avoid or otherwise compensate for significant impacts to fish and wildlife.

OBJECTIVE 3.9: Foster International Collaboration for Landscape Conservation

To fully succeed in conserving the fish and wildlife resources for which we have responsibility in the face of accelerating climate change, we must look beyond our borders to the rest of North America, the western hemisphere and, indeed, the whole world. We believe that strategic landscape conservation—landscape conservation that factors in climate change as well as non-climate stressors—will be the key to conserving needed habitats beyond our borders, whether for migratory songbirds in Central America, jaguars along the U.S.-Mexican border, tigers in Southeast Asia, or elephants in Africa. We will foster international landscape conservation on the North American continent by working through the Trilateral Committee, the Western Hemisphere Migratory Species Initiative, the Wildlife Without Borders[s] regional programs for Mexico and for Latin America and the Caribbean, and the Neotropical Migratory Bird Conservation Act grants program. In other regions of the world, we will work through our Wildlife Without Borders and Migratory Bird programs to promote landscape conservation to reduce climate change effects on priority species and landscapes.

---

[s] **Wildlife Without Borders** is the overarching title of the Division of International Conservation's species, regional and global conservation efforts. The Division of International Conservation is a component of the Service's International Affairs Program.

GOAL 4

We will develop monitoring and research partnerships that make available complete and objective information to plan, deliver, evaluate, and improve actions that facilitate fish and wildlife adaptation to accelerating climate change.

OBJECTIVE 4.1: Develop a National Biological Inventory and Monitoring Partnership

Biological inventory and monitoring are essential tools to understand the status and trends of fish and wildlife, as well as to help determine large-scale patterns of ecosystem health and response to climate change. To address this need, we will lead efforts to develop a national, integrated inventory and monitoring partnership to monitor continental changes in key populations and biological diversity. Our efforts will be driven by the inventory and monitoring priorities developed by LCCs and the National Wildlife Refuge System, as detailed in the Refuge System's draft *Strategic Plan for Inventories and Monitoring on National Wildlife Refuges: Adapting to Environmental Change,* as well as priorities developed collaboratively among many agencies within a National Fish and Wildlife Adaptation Strategy. We will leverage our efforts with those of existing Federal monitoring programs with proven track records and relevance to climate change (e.g., the National Park Service's Inventory and Monitoring Program, the Forest Service's Forest Inventory and Analysis Program, and the U.S. Geological Survey's National Phenology Network).

We will work with such partners as the U.S. Geological Survey and the National Aeronautics and Space Administration to define and implement remote-sensing monitoring programs for key biotic resources (e.g., vegetative cover, invasive species spread, wildfire frequency and aerial extent, plant phenology and primary productivity). We will support existing remote-sensing monitoring programs that have proven track records and are relevant to climate change (e.g., Terrestrial Observation and Prediction System).

We will incorporate new inventory and monitoring approaches as necessary and practical to achieve our goals.

OBJECTIVE 4.2: Promote Abiotic Monitoring Programs

Monitoring of abiotic resources and their change will be a key component of a comprehensive national monitoring program, particularly for larger landscapes. Within the National Wildlife Refuge System, we will: (1) work with partners to identify key abiotic resources that should be monitored, and assemble key existing abiotic data sets needed by Refuge System managers for comprehensive conservation planning; and (2) complete baseline hydrogeomorphic analyses at selected refuges (see the Refuge System's draft *Strategic Plan for Inventories and Monitoring on National Wildlife Refuges: Adapting to Environmental Change*).

We will work with such partners as the U.S. Geological Survey, the National Oceanic and Atmospheric Administration, and the National Aeronautics and Space Administration to define and implement abiotic remote-sensing monitoring priorities. We will support existing physical science and remote-sensing monitoring programs that have proven track records and are relevant to climate change (e.g., Remote Automated Weather Stations and the Terrestrial Observation and Prediction System).

OBJECTIVE 4.3: Develop Research and Monitoring Capability for Use in Landscape Conservation

Monitoring and research are key components of the Service's SHC framework. By measuring the effect of conservation efforts against explicitly predicted outcomes, managers can learn from both success and failure, thereby increasing the probability of success in future actions. By identifying uncertainties and assumptions in the models we use to develop biological objectives, we can prioritize and target key uncertainties and assumptions for research. We will develop appropriate research and monitoring capability, primarily within LCCs, to ensure that the adaptation efforts we undertake within the SHC framework are evaluated and that key uncertainties and assumptions are addressed through targeted research. We will provide relevant education and training opportunities to Service managers and ensure that this research and monitoring component is incorporated into all of our landscape conservation efforts.

Strategic Goals & Objectives

OBJECTIVE 4.4: Further Develop
Collaborative Research Partnerships

We will enhance existing and develop new collaborative partnerships to conduct research related to fish and wildlife adaptation to climate change. We will enhance our existing research partnerships at the Federal level, especially with the U.S. Geological Survey, the National Aeronautics and Space Administration, and the National Oceanic and Atmospheric Administration; with universities and university consortiums (e.g., Cooperative Ecosystem Studies Units); and with the private sector to design and implement a climate change research program in conjunction with LCCs and Climate Science Centers. We will develop new research partnerships as our needs dictate.

We have designated areas on National Wildlife Refuges as sites for long-term, integrated research and monitoring. These include Research Natural Areas (on 97 refuges) and Land Management and Research Demonstration Areas (on eight refuges). We will investigate expanding both these systems to achieve our climate change research and monitoring goals. The Refuge System's draft *Strategic Plan for Inventories and Monitoring on National Wildlife Refuges: Adapting to Environmental Change* calls for Research Natural Areas to be distributed among refuges over two strata — areas that are predicted to remain the same (i.e., climate refugia) and those predicted to have extremely dynamic climatic niches with uncertain outcomes. Additional Land Management and Research Demonstration Areas could be established in refuges to demonstrate adaptive management approaches to climate change and/or to serve as research sites for climate studies. We will direct additional funding, as it becomes available, to the Land Management and Research Demonstration Areas for climate change research.

Mitigation

GOAL 5

We will change our business practices to achieve carbon neutrality by the Year 2020.

OBJECTIVE 5.1: Assess and Reduce the Carbon Footprint of the Service's Facilities, Vehicles, Workforce, and Operations

We are committed as an agency to achieving carbon neutrality by the Year 2020. This will require that we reduce the energy use and carbon footprint of our buildings, facilities, vehicle fleet, workforce, and operations to the maximum extent possible. We have established a Carbon Neutral Team to carry out our ongoing efforts, to inventory, monitor, and evaluate our energy usage. By implementing best practices such as those identified in Service policy, expanding these efforts, and embarking upon new and innovative efforts across the Service, we anticipate success in reducing our carbon footprint by 5–10 percent annually between now and 2020. Example strategies are managing our fleet through life-cycle planning, including provisions in facility agreements and leases that promote conservation of energy and water, and ensuring that energy-related deferred maintenance activities are identified in the Service Asset Maintenance Management System. We anticipate that the reductions achieved, combined with our carbon sequestration and, perhaps, offsets, will lead us to carbon neutrality by 2020.

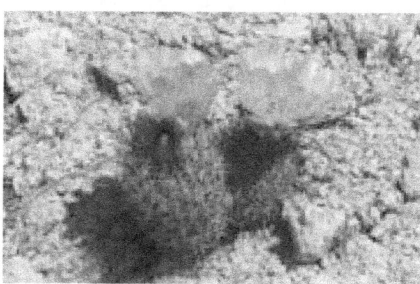

As the most readily recognized component of arid ecosystems, we intuitively think that cacti are uniquely adapted to live in the desert and may be able to withstand hotter and drier conditions brought on by climate change. Based on monitoring information we have collected for several Federally listed and candidate cacti species in Arizona and New Mexico, this may be an incorrect assumption. Populations of these cacti have been monitored for at least 20 years, with each species' population showing declines in overall numbers and reduced, or no, reproduction since the 1990s.

What will happen to these cacti species if drought conditions continue? Seed banks may be reduced, and seed germination and seedling survival will likely be reduced. Even for established plants, increases in rabbit and rodent predation of cacti that occur during drought may remove large, reproductive individual plants from populations.

Due to their limited geographic distribution, these cacti species may not be able to disperse into areas where they can persist. The management questions before us are, "How do we manage for these and similar species under changing climatic regimes?" and "Are these species candidates for population augmentation in their existing locations or for assisted colonization — moving them or placing seeds in other areas that may be favorable for their continued existence?"

MIMA FALK, *plant ecologist, Phoenix Ecological Services Field Office, Tucson, AZ*

(Above) Acuna cactus in bloom.
Photo: USFWS

OBJECTIVE 5.2: Assess and Reduce the Service's Land Management Carbon Footprint

The Service's land-management activities for wildlife have an associated carbon footprint. To achieve carbon neutrality, we must assess and reduce this footprint to the maximum extent possible while still achieving the Service's mission. Because our understanding of the carbon footprint associated with our land management activities is incomplete, the first step will be to inventory, monitor, and evaluate our emissions of greenhouse gases through these activities. We will then be in a position to consider how to reduce emissions while we achieve the Service's highest land-management priorities, a process that will involve evaluating green energy alternatives, considering trade-offs, and making difficult choices.

OBJECTIVE 5.3: Offset the Remaining Carbon Balance

After we minimize the carbon footprint of the Service's facilities, vehicles, operations, and land-management activities, a residual carbon footprint may remain. We will offset our residual carbon footprint through carbon sequestration and other measures, such as buying offsets, to become carbon neutral by the Year 2020.

GOAL 6

To conserve and restore fish and wildlife habitats at landscape scales while simultaneously sequestering atmospheric greenhouse gases, we will build our capacity to understand, apply, and share biological carbon sequestration science; and we will work with partners to implement carbon sequestration projects in strategic locations.

OBJECTIVE 6.1: Develop Biological Carbon Sequestration Expertise

Biological carbon sequestration has the potential to simultaneously accomplish both adaptation and mitigation objectives. For example, by reforesting a corridor between two protected areas with an appropriate mix of native trees, we not only sequester carbon, we create viable habitat as well. When the restored habitat contributes to attainment of explicit population objectives for climate-vulnerable species or species assemblages, then we are achieving both mitigation and adaptation objectives.

To accomplish this dual vision within priority landscapes, we will need to develop specific expertise in biological carbon sequestration through a Carbon Sequestration Working Group. We will then apply that expertise through the biological plans and conservation designs developed by LCCs. This expertise will be used to foster habitat restoration and carbon sequestration in key locations, such as National Wildlife Refuge System lands; and priority landscapes, such as the Lower Mississippi Valley.

OBJECTIVE 6.2: Develop Standards, Guidelines, and Best Management Practices for Biological Carbon Sequestration

The Carbon Sequestration Working Group will identify scientific approaches, standards, guidelines, and best management practices for biological carbon sequestration activities to achieve optimal fish and wildlife habitat through strict requirements for use of native vegetation. This information will be shared domestically and internationally to encourage large-scale partnerships in science-driven, biological carbon sequestration that supports fish and wildlife adaptation to climate change.

OBJECTIVE 6.3: Integrate Biological Carbon Sequestration Activities into Landscape Conservation Approaches

We will work to ensure that biological carbon sequestration activities, whether initiated by the Service or others, are implemented within an adaptive, landscape-conservation context. Applying our SHC framework, including biological planning and conservation design, on-the-ground delivery, and research and monitoring to evaluate success, LCCs will help us work with partners to determine where, when, how much, and what types of habitat should be conserved, protected, and enhanced in a given area to achieve both species and carbon-sequestration objectives.

OBJECTIVE 6.4: Facilitate Biological Carbon Sequestration Internationally

One of our most important roles in carbon sequestration may well be to facilitate habitat conservation through biological carbon sequestration at the international level. By working with international partners and stakeholders to help reduce deforestation rates in key areas, such as tropical forests; and by providing technical assistance and funding for carbon sequestration through reforestation, we will help preserve areas critical to biodiversity conservation and support greenhouse gas mitigation. We will work through our Wildlife Without Borders and Multinational Species programs to provide funding and technical assistance for projects designed to increase carbon sequestration, restore habitat, and increase habitat connectivity internationally.

OBJECTIVE 6.5: Facilitate Biological Carbon Sequestration Research

There are still gaps in our understanding of biological carbon sequestration and its benefits for wildlife habitat, especially in regard to wetlands and grasslands. Our carbon sequestration experts and managers will work with others, such as the U.S. Geological Survey, to identify and fill information gaps regarding biological carbon sequestration.

Section 712 of the Energy Independence and Security Act of 2007 mandates the Department of the Interior to develop a methodology and assess the capacity of our nation's ecosystems for ecological carbon sequestration and greenhouse gas flux mitigation. Secretarial Order 3289 implements the DOI Carbon Storage Project, with the U.S. Geological Survey as lead agency. The U.S. Geological Survey has initiated the LandCarbon Project to develop a methodology that meets specific Energy Independence and Security Act requirements. The Service will collaborate with the U.S. Geological Survey in the implementation of the methodology on Service lands.

OBJECTIVE 6.6: Evaluate Geologic Carbon Sequestration

Geologic carbon sequestration is the isolation and/or removal of carbon dioxide from industrial processes and its long-term storage underground to reduce or prevent increasing levels of carbon dioxide in the atmosphere.[15] The Department owns or has a material interest in more than 500 million acres of land in the United States, including National Wildlife Refuges. Beneath some of these lands exists the potential to sequester carbon dioxide in oil and gas reservoirs, deep saline reservoirs, and un-mineable coal seams. The Department may undertake an inventory of geologic carbon sequestration potential on its lands and may conduct research on the feasibility and environmental risks associated with geologic sequestration. We will participate in the Department's geologic carbon sequestration efforts to help ensure that potential impacts to fish and wildlife are considered and minimized.

Engagement

GOAL 7

We will engage Service employees; our local, State, Tribal, national, and international partners in the public and private sectors; our key constituencies and stakeholders; and everyday citizens in a new era of collaborative conservation in which, together, we seek solutions to the impacts of climate change and other 21st century stressors of fish and wildlife.

OBJECTIVE 7.1: Provide Service Employees with Climate Change Information, Education, and Training

Climate change is ushering in a new era of conservation for the Service that involves novel ways of thinking and bold innovations in the way we do business. We will view all of our endeavors through the lens of climate change and be willing to question the status quo, re-examine priorities and make difficult choices regarding where we can make a difference and where we cannot. We will communicate our climate change Strategic Plan to employees Service-wide. Every employee will be challenged to be engaged and to contribute to the plan's development and implementation. Our highly dedicated employees and our field-based organizational structure are our core strengths in addressing the impacts of climate change on wildlife resources. Building awareness within our workforce about the challenges and threats from a changing climate and developing the expertise to address these impacts are priorities.

Our External Affairs program and National Conservation Training Center will develop and implement a comprehensive employee engagement strategy addressing internal needs for information, education, and training about climate change. The plan will be aimed at ensuring every Service employee understands basic climate change science, the urgency of the climate change challenge to our mission, and what actions each of us can take professionally and personally to engage in mitigation and adaptation activities.

The National Conservation Training Center will develop and implement a climate change curriculum to train Service employees in methods to address climate change in their day-to-day activities. The training will also prepare our employees to serve as a resource for our partners, stakeholders, and the public as these groups engage in climate change adaptation and mitigation activities. The National Conservation Training Center will incorporate climate change information from this curriculum into other course offerings as appropriate.

OBJECTIVE 7.2: Share Climate Change Information, Education, and Training Opportunities with External Audiences

To effectively address climate change nationally, every conservation partner must be both a learner and a teacher. As we in the Service learn, we will also step up to fulfill our teaching role with our national and international partners, our stakeholders, our key constituencies, and the public, anticipating that they will do the same for us. To accomplish our teaching

role, our External Affairs program and National Conservation Training Center will develop and implement, in conjunction with programs and regions, a comprehensive engagement strategy for external information, education, and communication about climate change. The plan will help to create a broad-scale awareness of the urgent nature of the effects of accelerating climate change on fish and wildlife and habitats; and will engage others in becoming part of the solution through such means as minimizing their carbon footprints.

The National Conservation Training Center will work with the Refuge System and the Fisheries program to develop climate change materials and provide informational, educational, and training opportunities to external audiences, using the National Wildlife Refuge System, National Fish Hatcheries, the Service website, and employee presentations as primary venues for this engagement with the public.

To become a better, more informed partner, we will actively seek knowledge from State, Federal, Tribal, and local government agencies; non-governmental organizations; business and industry already engaged in addressing climate change; and individual citizens. We will put the same energy into learning from others as we do teaching others what we know.

We will provide technical assistance to public and private landowners, conservation organizations, business and industry, and governments at all levels to help them understand impacts to fish, wildlife and habitats as a result of climate change; and to encourage them to undertake adaptation, mitigation, and engagement activities to address those impacts.

OBJECTIVE 7.3: Forge Alliances and Create Forums on Climate Change to Exchange Information and Knowledge and to Influence International Policy

Working principally through our International Affairs and Migratory Birds programs, we will engage other countries in sharing state-of-the-art knowledge on climate change adaptation, mitigation, and education strategies. We will seek to learn from their experiences and will share our experiences with them to achieve a common understanding and common ground for moving forward together on climate change policy and action. We will also seek ways to address climate change more effectively through the United Nations Framework Convention on Climate Change; international conventions, such as the Convention on International Trade in Endangered Species of Wild Fauna and Flora, the Convention on Wetlands of International Importance (Ramsar Convention), and other international agreements.

By also engaging with our international partners and foreign governments in informing and educating their citizens about the causes and consequences of climate change, the Service will have an opportunity to further wildlife adaptation and climate change mitigation around the world. With our partners, we will help to create worldwide support for minimizing deforestation and for creating new habitat through carbon sequestration activities; and we will encourage local community participation in international carbon markets that reduce greenhouse gas emissions.

Rising to the Challenge

OUR PLAN IS AMBITIOUS — RIGHTFULLY AND NECESSARILY SO. When it comes to climate change, we cannot afford a failure of imagination. If we are to accomplish our vital mission of "working with others to conserve, protect, and enhance fish, wildlife, and plants and their habitats for the continuing benefit of the American people," addressing the greatest threat to that mission — climate change — must be our highest priority.

We must treat climate change as the national security issue that it is. Going forward, we must dedicate our energies, our resources, and our creativity to a long-term campaign to reduce emissions of greenhouse gases as a first line of attack in a battle against an enemy that threatens the sustainability of fish and wildlife populations, the viability of ecosystems, and the well-being of every citizen. We must mobilize efforts to help fish and wildlife adapt to changes that have already occurred in their habitats as a result of climate change, and changes that we foresee in the future. We must confront climate change as a communal problem, engaging all segments of society as partners and potential partners. We must implement our Strategic Plan and 5-Year Action Plan, reaching inward to every part of our organization and outward to the larger conservation community to build the will, the relationships, the capabilities and the resources we need to succeed.

We will carry out our responsibilities with humility and gratitude — humility in recognizing how much we have yet to learn about climate change and its impacts on wildlife; and gratitude that if we act now, it is not too late to do something about it. We honor our employees for the important strides they have already made in addressing climate change on the ground before Service plans were formalized, and we will build on those efforts. We respect our conservation partners for the ways in which they are taking action to address climate change as organizations and as individuals, and we will join our efforts with theirs.

As daunting as the issue of climate change may seem, we accept that every generation has faced environmental challenges, and this is ours to deal with. We will remember those conservation heroes upon whose shoulders we stand, and like them, we will rise up to confront the conservation challenge of our day with courage and resolve. We will move forward with enthusiasm and optimism borne of confidence in the soundness of the plans we have created, in the ingenuity of our workforce, and in the results we will achieve in collaboration with our partners. We will remain inspired by keeping the future of fish and wildlife at the forefront of our thinking. And we will look forward to that day when we can speak of climate change as yesterday's crisis.

We stand now where two roads diverge. But unlike the roads in Robert Frost's familiar poem, they are not equally fair. The road we have long been traveling is deceptively easy, a smooth superhighway on which we progress with great speed, but at its end lies disaster. The other fork of the road / the one less traveled by / offers our last, our only chance to reach a destination that assures the preservation of the earth.

RACHEL CARSON (1907–1964), world-famous environmentalist, celebrated author, and one-time employee of the U.S. Fish and Wildlife Service

Literature Cited

1 Intergovernmental Panel on Climate Change. 2007. Climate Change 2007: Synthesis Report. Contribution of Working Groups I, II and III to the Fourth Assessment Report of the Intergovernmental Panel on Climate Change [Core Writing Team, Pachauri, R.K and Reisinger, A. (eds.)]. IPCC, Geneva, Switzerland. 104 pp.

2 Backlund, P., A. Janetos, and D. Schimel (convening lead authors). 2008. The effects of climate change on agriculture, land resources, water resources, and biodiversity in the United States. Synthesis and Assessment Product 4.3. Report by the U.S. Climate Change Science Program and the Subcommittee on Global Change Research. U.S. Environmental Protection Agency, Washington, D.C. 362 pp.

3 US Fish and Wildlife Service. 2008. Determination of threatened status for the polar bear (*Ursus maritimus*) throughout its range. Federal Register Vol. 73:28212-28303. May 15, 2008.

4 McLaughlin, J.F., J.J. Hellmann, C.L. Boggs, and P.R. Ehrlich. 2002. Climate change hastens population extinctions. Proceedings of the National Academy of Sciences 99:6070-6074.

5 Both, C., S. Bouwhuis, C.M. Lessells, and M.E. Visser. 2006. Climate change and population declines in a long-distance migratory bird. Nature 414:81-83.

6 Field, C.B., L.D. Mortsch, M. Brklacich, D.L. Forbes, P. Kovacs, J.A. Patz, S.W. Running and M.J. Scott. 2007. North America. Climate Change 2007: Impacts, Adaptation and Vulnerability. Contribution of Working Group II to the Fourth Assessment Report of the Intergovernmental Panel on Climate Change. M.L. Parry, O.F. Canziani, J.P. Palutikof, P.J. van der Linden, and C.E. Hanson, (eds.) IPCC, Geneva, Switzerland. Pages 617-652.

7 Glick, P., J. Clough, and B. Nunley. 2008. Sea level rise and coastal habitats in the Chesapeake Bay region. Technical Report. National Wildlife Federation, Washington, DC. 121 pp.

8 National Ecological Assessment Team (NEAT). 2006. Strategic Habitat Conservation: Final Report of the National Ecological Assessment Team. July 2006. "45 pp.

9 Runge, M. 2008. Strategic Habitat Conservation: Making sense of acronyms. Refuge Update 5(3):10-11.

10 Millar, C.I., N.L. Stephenson, and S.L. Stephens. 2007. Climate change and forests of the future: Managing in the face of uncertainty. Ecological Applications 17(8):2145-2151.

11 Galatowitsch, S., L. Frelich, and L. Phillips-Mao. 2009. Regional climate change adaptation strategies for biodiversity conservation in a midcontinental region of North America. Biological Conservation 142:2012-2022.

12 Choi, Y.D. 2007. Restoration ecology to the future: A call for new paradigm. Restoration Ecology 15(2):351-353.

13 Mawdsley, J.R., R. O'Malley, and D.S. Ojima. 2009. A review of climate-change adaptation strategies for wildlife management and biodiversity conservation. Conservation Biology 23(5):1080-1089.

14 Beier, P., and B. Brost. 2010. Use of land facets to plan for climate change: Conserving the arenas, not the actors. Conservation Biology 24(3):701-710.

15 Department of the Interior Task Force on Climate Change. 2008. An analysis of climate change impacts and options relevant to the Department of the Interior's managed lands and waters: Report of the subcommittee on land and water management. Department of the Interior, Washington, DC. 150 pp.

The mission of the U.S. Fish and Wildlife
Service is working with others to
conserve, protect and enhance fish,
wildlife, plants and their habitats for the
continuing benefit of the American people.
We are both a leader and trusted partner
in fish and wildlife conservation,
known for our scientific excellence,
stewardship of lands and natural
resources, dedicated professionals and
commitment to public service.

For more information on our work
and the people who make it happen,
visit <www.fws.gov>.

September 2010

www.ingramcontent.com/pod-product-compliance
Lightning Source LLC
Chambersburg PA
CBHW081135280526
45787CB00007B/3097